Crabapples

Nicola's floating home

Bobbie Kalman

Crabtree Publishing Company

Crabapples

created by Bobbie Kalman

For Nicola, Sascha, Samantha, Christl, and George Hill

Editor-in-Chief
Bobbie Kalman

Managing editor
Lynda Hale

Editors
Petrina Gentile
Niki Walker
Tammy Everts
Greg Nickles
Natalie Bullard

Computer design
Lynda Hale

Cover design
David T. Cole

Illustrations
Barb Bedell: pages 22-23

Special thanks to
Jessica Lindal who appears on pages 5, 12, 28, and 30;
Lynda Hale, whose assistance on Harbour Island was invaluable
in coordinating the photo research and photo shoot

Photographs
Photographs of Nicola as a young child are the property
of the Hill family.
All current photographs of Nicola and her family were taken
by Bobbie Kalman and Peter Crabtree except the following:
Lynda Hale: page 32
Christopher Hartley: page 29 (left)
Christl Hill: title page

Color separations and film
Dot 'n Line Image Inc.

Printer
Worzalla Publishing Company

Crabtree Publishing Company

350 Fifth Avenue
Suite 3308
New York
N.Y. 10118

360 York Road, RR 4,
Niagara-on-the-Lake,
Ontario, Canada
L0S 1J0

73 Lime Walk
Headington
Oxford OX3 7AD
United Kingdom

Cataloging in Publication Data
Kalman, Bobbie, 1947-
    Nicola's floating home

(Crabapples)
Includes index.
ISBN 0-86505-626-9 (library bound)   ISBN 0-86505-726-5 (pbk.)
This book describes the life of Nicola, a ten-year-old girl who
lives on a sailboat.

1. Hill, Nicola - Juvenile literature. 2. Seafaring life - Juvenile
literature. 3. Sailboats - Juvenile literature. 4. Boats and
boating - Juvenile literature. I. Title. II. Series: Kalman,
Bobbie, 1947-   . Crabapples.

GV811.65.K35 1995   j797.1'24   LC 95-35940
                                                        CIP

What is in this book?

Meet Nicola

Nicola Hill was born in Reading, England. When she was a year old, her parents decided to spend more time with their children. The family began a long sailing adventure! Nicola is now ten. She has visited many exciting places around the world. Wherever she travels, she makes good friends.

The photographs in this book were taken at different times in Nicola's life. The picture on the top left of the opposite page shows Nicola and her sister Samantha just after they moved onto their boat. In the picture with the kitten, Nicola is ten.

This book is about living on a boat and visiting new places. It is also about an adventurous girl who loves people and animals.

Nicola's family

Nicola lives with her parents, Christl and George, and her brother Sascha. Sascha is now 16. Her older sister Samantha, shown here as a teenager, no longer lives at home. She works as a crew member on a big boat.

The Hills are a close family. They enjoy being together. They depend on one another to sail the boat. Sascha and Samantha have helped look after Nicola since she was a baby. They played with her and taught her how to swim.

Nicola's mother is her teacher, nurse, and friend. Together they enjoy playing cards, going in-line skating, pressing flowers, and cooking. Christl takes Nicola skiing when they visit her family in Austria.

When on shore, Nicola and her father often go on nature walks. At night, they try to spot **constellations** and bright navigation stars. George also teaches Nicola how to sail the boat and steer the dinghy. He takes Nicola deep-sea diving. She did her first dive in France at the age of three!

Kirtonia

Nicola's floating home is a sailboat called Kirtonia. It is 58 feet (18 meters) long and 16 feet (5 meters) at its widest point. The Hills have sailed Kirtonia throughout the Mediterranean and Caribbean seas and across the Atlantic Ocean.

The **mast** holds up the **mainsail**.

The **jib** is a sail at the bow.

Ropes are called **lines**, **sheets**, or **halyards**.

The front of the boat is the **bow.**

The **deck** is the top floor.

The back of the boat is the **stern.**

The **hull** is the body of the boat.

The **cockpit** contains a table, benches, storage lockers, and the **helm**, or wheel.

To steer the boat, Nicola turns the helm to move the **rudder** at the stern.

Below deck

The stairway from the deck to the **saloon** is the **companionway**.

Nicola's floating home is large and comfortable. Below deck, it is similar to a house on land. There is a living room, a kitchen, four bedrooms, two bathrooms, and plenty of closets and cupboards. On a boat, rooms, closets, windows, clothing, stairs, and supplies all have **nautical** names.

Nicola brushes her teeth in the bathroom, or **head**.

She peeks down from the deck into her cabin through a **hatch**.

This chart will help you learn the names for the different parts of a boat:

living and dining area	**saloon**
kitchen	**galley**
bedroom	**cabin**
bathroom	**head**
side window	**porthole**
window to deck	**hatch**
cupboard or closet	**locker**
stairs	**companionway**
bed	**bunk**
equipment and clothing	**gear**

Nicola has a **hanging locker** for storing her **gear**.

The **galley** has **fiddles** to keep food from sliding off the shelves.

The saloon is the living area. How many **portholes** do you see?

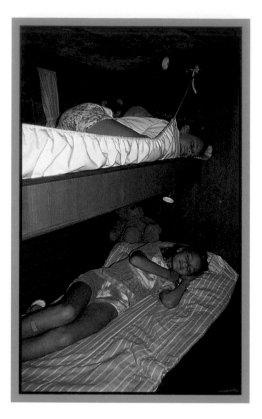

Everyday life

In many ways, Nicola's life is like yours. Her father wakes her up at eight o'clock each morning, and Nicola goes to bed at nine o'clock at night. Each day, she does schoolwork and chores. In her spare time, Nicola reads, draws, plays with her toys, and watches television. She also loves to have sleep-overs with friends.

Chores galore

There is always a lot of work to be done on Kirtonia. Sascha changes the oil in the boat's main engine and **generator** and helps his father with repairs that need to be done.

Sascha also cleans the bottom of the boat when seaweed grows on it. Sometimes sea worms cling to his legs while he is underwater!

Nicola raises the flag in the morning and lowers it at sunset. She coils the ropes, called sheets, around **winches** to keep them tidy.

Nicola also cleans her cabin, makes her bunk, sets and clears the table, helps with the dishes, and hangs out the laundry to dry. One of her favorite chores is helping with the cooking. Nicola loves making pancakes.

School time!

Nicola's father says the world is Nicola's school, and it is! Each time the Hills sail to a new country, Nicola learns about the history and customs of the people who live there.

Nicola goes on nature walks and reads about the plants and animals she has seen. She presses the flowers she finds to preserve them. Using her diving gear, she explores coral reefs in the sea.

Each day, Nicola has two hours of lessons on the boat. Her parents are her teachers. She also reads on her own and practices math and language skills on the computer.

Getting dinner

The Hills eat wonderful meals on the boat. Sascha and Nicola often catch fish for dinner. Once they caught a huge tuna that weighed more than Sascha! They also climb trees to pick local fruit. Sascha has to reach for that coconut.

The Hills buy fresh food when they can. They do not have to shop every day because there is a freezer on Kirtonia.

Water and electricity

When you need water, you turn on the tap.
If a room is dark, you flip a switch to turn
on the light. On Kirtonia, you cannot take
water or electricity for granted because
both are made on the boat.

Diesel fuel runs the generator, which makes electricity. A special machine filters the salt out of ocean water so the Hills can use it for drinking and bathing.

It takes a lot of time and fuel to make electricity and fresh water. The Hills are always careful to conserve both.

Instead of using a dryer, they hang their laundry to dry. They switch off lights that are not in use. They take quick showers and turn off the water while they brush their teeth.

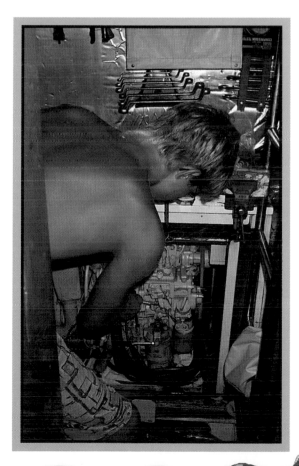

The Hills are careful about their garbage, as well. They buy only things they need. They prefer fresh food to packaged food, so they throw away very little garbage.

Eye on the weather

When you are on a boat, it is very important to know when storms are on the way. Sascha has just received a satellite picture of the weather. The winds are high. To be safe, his father suggests they pull up anchor and **dock** Kirtonia.

Kirtonia has a complete **navigation station** on board. It includes a computer, radio, radar, and **weather fax**. When the Hills are sailing, George uses charts and a **pilot's book** to find out where the reefs and currents are in the waters ahead.

Sometimes George asks a local **pilot** to **navigate** his boat. Local pilots know when the sands shift and the water is too shallow for big boats. Edsel, the pilot below, navigated Kirtonia through the Devil's Backbone in the Bahamas.

Accidents can happen

On a boat, safety is a matter of life and death! There is a large first-aid kit on Kirtonia. Each cabin has a fire extinguisher and smoke detector. A dinghy, life jackets, life rings, flares, and safety harnesses are all on board. When Nicola was a baby, her parents put netting around the boat to keep her from falling off.

Although the Hills take great care to be safe, accidents can happen. When Nicola was eight, her mother had a terrible accident while the family was out on the ocean. Both her arms were caught in an electric winch that kept turning when it should have stopped. All the bones in her right arm were broken.

Quick action saved Christl's life. George ran below to turn off the main power and call the coast guard. Sascha comforted Christl.

It took a half hour for the helicopter to arrive and take Christl to a hospital. She was ill for many months. Nicola still has nightmares about the accident!

Boating Friends

When the Hills arrive at a new **port**, they get to know the people whose boats are docked there. Boating people are very friendly. They share food, information, and supplies. They help one another with boat repairs. The children have fun playing. Sometimes several boats sail together to the next port. It is safer and more fun than sailing alone.

Great times!

You might think Nicola spends most of her time on the boat, but that is far from true. Kirtonia is not just a home. It is also transportation. The Hills have sailed Kirtonia to exciting places all over the world. When they arrive at a new place, they see the sights, shop, or go swimming.

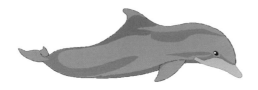

There is never a dull moment when you travel from place to place. Each day is like a holiday! Flying on a trapeze, climbing a tree with a friend, playing at the bottom of the ocean, or swimming with dolphins can be part of a day's activities. Snorkeling, deep-sea diving, and windsurfing are also favorite pastimes for the Hills.

Saying good-bye

One of the hardest things about living on a boat is saying good-bye to new friends. Nicola cried when her friend Jessica had to go home to Canada, but the two friends are now penpals!